Walking Down Awen's Path:
Working with Divine Inspiration

by David P. Smith

ISBN 978-1-61392-045-9
First edition: February 2013

Oaklight Publishing
4306 Independence Street
Rockville, MD 20853USA

For Frederick, Christen, and Charlie: may Awen's inspiration fill your life. With special thanks to Mother Nature and all the people and artistic expressions that have inspired me.

Special thanks to
Damh the Bard
and
James Maertens
for their input.

Table of Contents

Foreward

Awen is the Welsh word for "poetic inspiration." To modern druids, the word signifies something deeper and more holy than is usually meant by the word "inspiration." As Thomas Edison said, in reference to inventing the light bulb, "Invention is one percent inspiration and ninety-nine percent perspiration." What he did not say was that without the one percent, the seed of illumination and imagination to start the process, all the perspiration is likely to amount to nothing. For artists, inventors, and scientists -- indeed for all of us -- Awen is that moment of insight that we can never quite explain. An idea "just comes" to us. Or suddenly we "see the light."

We speak often of "breakthroughs" in the field of invention, and certainly the phenomenon is also a part of creating poetry or art of any kind. But what is it we are breaking through? Our mental block?

Rather, I suggest, it is something breaking through to us from a different plane of reality. Inspiration is a moment of enlightenment, when the "block" of our ordinary everyday consciousness suddenly becomes a doorway and the light from that higher realm breaks in upon our minds. This is the process Rev. David Smith introduces in the book you are holding. As the titled suggests, to engage with Awen, with inspiration, is a journey, a path one must walk down, a life experience.

Awen is something "outside" us and "inside" us, but becoming aware of it in both of these senses, we realize that "inside" and "outside" are illusions that dissolve when we see the world on the deep level of spirit. Deeper in the sense of underlying what exists. Higher in the sense that we usually think of this state of consciousness as a "higher" state because we can see more and further, as if we were standing on a mountainside. Walking Awen's path is our walk through the world, but seeing more, seeing the connections of all things with each other as we walk. Seeing connections is the root of creative inspiration, as it is the universal truth of all religions. The "thousand things" of the visible and invisible worlds are woven together like a spider's web -- touch one strand and the others all vibrate.

The exercises and meditations in Rev. Smith's book will guide you to first discover that Awen is something you already possess, something that flows through you even if you think you could never write a poem to save your life. He shows how taking time to be in nature, just observing and connecting with something as simple as the cycle of the seasons will open your mind to the three luminous rays of Awen. Like the three drops of the brew of knowledge that fell on the finger of Gwion Bach and transformed him into the great Cymric poet Taliesin, the three rays of the traditional symbol for Awen resonate symbolically like the plucked strings of a harp.

Three rays of light symbolizing the three syllables of the divine word of creation. Three rays emblematical of the sun's light at the solstices and the equinoxes. These in turn themselves expressing the point of balance between light and darkness, the brilliance of Summer's long days and the contemplative grey of Winter's short days. In one extreme, we live in the daylight mostly, the awakened, thinking mind of consciousness. In the other extreme we live mostly asleep though the long darkness of night filled with

dreaming and the power of the Moon. At the equinoxes, our conscious and unconscious minds are at perfect balance. None of these points is better than the other. All are a part of how our minds and lives are made, how we live on this Earth within its seasons. Nature conditions the very structure and rhythm of our minds.

As Rev. Smith tells us here, Awen is also like the Hindu's prana, a force or substance coming to us from the Sun, a substance of light and life as well as vision. Like a sun- bather on a beach, we must relax and open ourselves to the lifegiving Sun, from which everything in nature is generated. The Sun is, in this sense, the Great Progenitor or Allfather. Read, but most important: Do. If you perform the exercises in this book, taking them slowly, you will feel your own unfolding and experience the inflowing of the Divine Imagination into our soul.

And this means discovering who you really are. Discovering where you are really going. Discovering the calling and the pathway of your unique and perfect life.

Alferian Gwydion MacLir Minneapolis, Minnesota November 2012

David P. Smith

/|\ 6

Author's Note

Within the pages of this book, you will find my take on Awen, as I have come to know it through years of study and practice. The meditations and exercises are things that have worked for myself and may work for you too. Please feel free to take from this what you like and disregard anything that does not fit your personal practices.

I hope that you will find working with Awen as rewarding and enriching as I have throughout my years of druidic practice.

Yours Under the Trees,

David P. Smith

David P. Smith

/|\ 8

Part 1: Awen as Inspiration

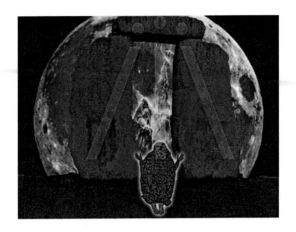

David P. Smith

Chapter 1: What is Awen?

/|\
"See me as the Sun on the mountaintop,
Feel me in the power of the seas.
Hear me in the laughter of the stream,
Power of nature, power of the trees."
("Song of Awen" by Damh the Bard)

Awen is the Welsh word meaning poetic inspiration, and has also come to represent the inspiration that flows through us all; it can also be seen as divine inspiration. It inspires art, music, poetry, actions, deeds, and is indeed magical. It is the spirit of life, of light, and of truth. The Awen is often represented by three rays of light; it is used as a sacred symbol and intoned as a sound by many Druids and Druid groups as a focus to bring forth the Awen which exists within.

The Awen symbol represents the sun on the equinoxes and solstices. It is the three drops of divine inspiration that came forth from the cauldron of Cerridwen, as in the story of Taliesin. Awen exists all around us—in all of nature—and is the source of our inspiration; it is a major guiding light on the path of enlightenment. It is the inspirational force used by nature, deity, the ancestors, and the inner guides to help guide and teach us along our paths.

It was from the three signs that Einigan the Giant obtained so good an understanding of letters, which he cut on staves. He devised the mode, and made twelve principal letters, if the books of the wise are true, which are called the ten radicals. As to what they are, and what their forms, it is a secret in the mystery of the Bards of the nation of the Cymry, namely, the Gwyddoniaid, who are called the primary Bards. They are three of the primary radicals, that is, the three cuttings; and they are called cuttings, because they are cut out of the dark into three rays; and for the same reason we say, the break of dawn, to cut a field, to cut or break out. The third break out was the voice of a song of triumph, that is, the first voice was a voice of triumph.

The three foundations of Awen from God: to understand the truth; to love the truth; and to [maintain] the truth, so that nothing may prevail against it. From these three things may the question be correctly answered--Why wouldest thou be a Bard? And from correctly answering the question is the degree of Chair obtained or refused. The answer is between the aspirant and his conscience, and between his conscience and God, not between him and his teacher."

In the introduction of The Welsh Question and Druidism, third edition by Griffith, it states "The mark /|\ has been adopted from time immemorial, long before the Christian Era, by the Welsh nation. It means the radiating light of intelligence, or the eye of light. It is sometimes called the 'three rods or rays of light,' and the 'three voices'; that is, the three voices of conscience."

When we are able to connect to Awen—to feel it, to see it, and to ride its tides of inspiration—then we can embrace the paths we are on; we can find the inner truth and light we seek. We are all beings of light; though encased in flesh, the flesh we are is not what makes us who we are. Awen allows us to connect with our spirit, our true being.

Awen helps us identify a longing for our paths; deepens our understanding of the paths which we follow; and it is a gift given to us by the universe, so we might have a deeper understanding of what and who we are. We have the ability to grow far beyond what we are—the power of Awen will help us to hear the song of creation, and we will find not only our true being but also our oneness with the universal whole. It is light and sound, it is finite and infinite, all at the same time.

Awen is an all-present inspirational force; it is not to be confused with Nwyfre, which is the life force or magical force that is within us all. They are different—yet interconnected—forces that help guide our spiritual development. Awen is a pathway to connection, and this connection kindles within us what the Celts called the "Fire in the Head."

Many creation myths speak of the use of sound: words being spoken, tales being told, songs being sung, and dances danced as the universe comes into being. One of the first creations in many of these myths is Light, which illuminated the darkness that had existed before creation. From this sound and this light, all creation comes forth and becomes part of the dynamic oneness—the universe—and the collective whole that exists everywhere.

The sun brings us light, heat, and energy; without it, we would not be able to exist. Around us the plants and animals sing their own songs, and with the light, they join to make the wonderful web of life that we live within. Each thread of the web connects with another; ultimately, all life is connected.

As each part of the web relies upon another part, all rely upon the light and song, which surround us all. What we must learn to do, if we are to grow as spiritual beings, is learn to reconnect with the natural world around us. We must learn to hear the song of creation and to see the light that shines to illuminate our paths. What we need is to find our way through the darkness and quagmire of illusion that exists around us. Awen can help us to do this and can illuminate the path that lies before us.

It does not matter if we wish to call it Awen, divine inspiration, spiritual guidance, the force, or a multitude of other terms. It does not matter what faith we call our own or what path we walk down. We must believe that we are beings of light—this is an important lesson—and as we grow and learn in this life, we also know that we are but a part of a large and glorious universe. Scientific theory and religious dogma can attempt to explain the origin of the universe; that is not the scope of this book. What is presented here is not dogma but universal truths, which can help anyone on any path. It is the firm belief of the author that although faith is extremely important in one's life and in finding the inspiration of Awen, the exact faith or dogma followed is not as long as universal themes and truths are accepted.

To connect with the world, with our fellow human beings, and with the universal whole is an extremely personal, lifelong task. What works for one person will not work for another; no matter how much we wish to tell someone our truth, each person must journey along his or her path to find the truth—no one can be told. Many paths lead to the universal truths and enlightenment. Awen can help guide us and strengthen us on our personal paths, but it cannot do the work alone. To truly connect, to find the truth and light we seek, we must be willing to follow our personal paths through work and practice—then we can truly learn to see the light and hear the song.

Awen is transmitted in so many ways—from the beauty of a flower to the Sun's warming rays. It is awe-inspiring to go out into nature and to see the flowing of Awen all around: to hear the song of the breeze through the trees, to hear the laughter of children at play, to listen to the birds as they chirp their tunes, and to your inner self as it bathes in the all-encompassing Awen.

Awen comes in flashes when it is ready, like all inspiration; meditation or other spiritual practices can also foster it and help it grow. Though there will be times when life becomes hectic, and it seems that the inspiration will have left or becomes blocked, it does come back and is usually stronger than before.

The inspiration brought forth by Awen is not purely artistic or poetical; it can also be quite spiritual. Awen, in its many forms, can inspire your spiritual development and practices. This is not tied to one particular faith; in fact, it can aid the spiritual development of anyone willing to be open to it.

Exercise 1: How Does Awen Touch You?

For this exercise you will need a piece of paper, notebook, or journal and a writing implement. Take a moment to think of times in your life when you felt deeply inspired—whether it was a flash of inspiration of what to do on a specific day, or an artistic, musical, or writing pursuit. Think about everything that was happening at the time.

Now write down what exactly inspired you.

What inspired your actions—was it music, nature, or an idea from another person? Write down everything you can think of; then, think about what seems to inspire you in general. Write that down; be sure to keep this to refer to later. If we know what inspires us, we have a critical tool in helping us work consciously with Awen.

Guided Meditation 1: Awakening the Awen Within.

Close your eyes. Now become aware of your breathing: in and out, in and out. Become aware of your body; start with your feet and work your way up to your head. As you become aware of each muscle and muscle group, feel them loosen and become completely relaxed. Pause for a moment and feel your body in its fully relaxed state.

Once you are completely relaxed, think back to a time when you felt inspired. It can be any form of inspiration—from the flash of an idea of what to do for dinner to the creation of a painting, poem, drawing, story, or song. Try to remember every detail you can about this time —the sights, the smells, the time of day, the sounds, and how you felt—and try your best to experience them again.

As you remember this event, you realize that this was a time you were touched by Awen. Now tap into the Awen energies of that time. When you feel you have experienced this moment as much as you can, allow yourself to become aware of your surroundings once more, of the here and now, and try to retain the feeling of Awen as you do. Now pick up a pencil and paper, or paints and canvas, or another medium you desire, and try to create something, anything that strikes your fancy. It does not have to be great—it can be anything to help you be part of the creative process—and let Awen flow through you in the here and now.

Once you are done, write down what happened during your meditation (a journal is a highly valuable tool for this work so you can look back and see your path as you have written it). Repeat this meditation anytime you wish; the more you practice the exercises and meditations in this book, the stronger you will feel a connection to Awen.

Chapter 2: Awen's Many Expressions

"I decided that it was not wisdom that enabled poets to write their poetry, but a kind of instinct or inspiration, such as you find in seers and prophets who deliver all their sublime messages without knowing in the least what they mean."
(Socrates)

In every work of art, every story, every poem that flows forth from the lips of the Bard, you can see Awen. The more you use it, the more it grows— it is a source of wisdom and a great friend to those of an artistic mind. Through the very act of creating art, in all its form, Awen is given birth and takes on a life of its own. It begins rather slow, and then starts to grow. From within, it brings forth the tales of Bards and the songs of the stars, whether consciously realized or not. When you consciously call forth the Awen within, it becomes a wondrous experience. In this creative state all things are possible; it sets ideal conditions for working magic. It is amazing to feel Awen flowing freely through you.

When it works through us, Awen brings us into the very process of creation. Whether we take the time to write poetry, draw, paint, sing, or compose, we are truly channeling and working with the wondrous Awen. It is through Awen that we truly find wisdom, and by working with it, we find the inspiration to go forth—to learn and to teach.

Awen can teach us through our own artistic

pursuits; it can also inspire us when we see or read others' works of art. Within the following pages are pictures of some of my paintings, ceramics, and poems, and some comments on them. I hope they inspire you in your own work, or perhaps teach you something. I also dabble with some nature and sacred-site photography, which you may find elsewhere in the book.

(The following two poems were inspired by a trip in 2006 to many of the sacred sites in England).

Chalice Well

From deep within her body it flows,Her blood passing through her bones,Flowing eternally without fail,Shed to nourish,While her children flourish,From high mountain to misty vale,We come to drink of her blood,From this place where starts the flood,Renewing our beings to our souls,Refreshing rejuvenating all,Whether we are large or small,Freeing us from our own controls,From human to beast,We are all released,From where the grail water flows.

Faerie Falls

The faeries fly round and round,As water falls to the ground,As the magic fills the air,Pilgrims make their offerings to the fae,Hoping and wishing with each passing day,The pristine glen with ancient magic,To mar this place would be tragic,The beauty of the paradise moves my very soul,Until I fell I've lost all control,

And am moved to sing along,I can hear the words of the trees,Carried on the cooling breeze,My heart soars above the falls,As deep within I hear the calls,The call to peace,And true release,My eyes flood with tears,Feeling the joy of many years,Happiness, peace, and soaring love,As the water falls down from above.

(The Following is a song I wrote while thinking about

Awen and how to speak of it.)

The Voice of the Awen

Hear the Voice of the Awen,

The sweet song that it sings,

Feel the Joy, the Power, the Inspiration

That it always brings.

See the Rays of the Awen

Shining through the trees,

Hear the Song of the Awen

Carried on the breeze.

Inspiring the Faithful

To go down on their knees.

Fill your soul with inspiration,

Brought forth by Mother Earth,

The gift given to us all,

At the moment of our birth.

Hear the voice of the Awen,

The lessons it can teach,

Know that there is nothing

That is beyond our reach.

Learn the Teachings of the Awen,

They will set you free

From the anger and self-doubt

That exists in you and me.

Give yourself to the Awen,

It will give itself to you,

And in the words of the immortal Bard,

"To thine own self be true."

Let the truth rule your life,

It will never lead you wrong,

Feel the power of Awen,

And its eternal song.

(The following pictures are of ceramics and a canvas I painted, which are either symbolic or teach some lesson. I will leave it to you to interpret these as you wish—hopefully they will teach something.)

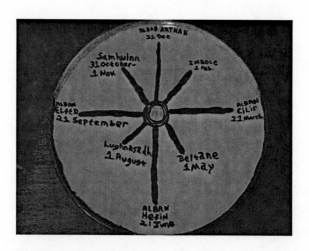

The Wheel of the Year

The Awen Plate

The Druid Plate

Triquetra Painting

When you work with Awen, it is vital you try to be in the now, the present, and let it flow freely. Be true to your inner self; Awen can teach you much and bring you wisdom. As stated by William Shakespeare (and it is still as true today as when he first penned it in *Hamlet*), "This above all: to thine own self be true." This is important to realize in spirituality as well as in everyday life.

Exercise 2: Working with Awen

Take a moment to clear your mind. Become aware of your breathing: in and out, in and out. Visualize three rays of light flowing down into your brow—entering your very being—and feel the rays warming and inspiring you. When you feel that you are filled with this inspiration, pick up a piece of paper and a pen. Write, draw, or do whatever comes to you. Create something, then sit back and look at what you have created. Did you write a poem or a story? Did you fold the paper into origami or cut it into a snowflake? Think about how you felt while you created this: are you pleased with what you created, or is it something you would like to work on more? Record your responses in your journal.

Guided Meditation 2: Three Rays Meditation

Close your eyes. Now become aware of your breathing: in and out, in and out. Become aware of your body; start with your feet and work your way up to your head. As you become aware of each muscle and muscle group, feel them loosen and become completely relaxed. Pause for a moment, and feel your body in its fully relaxed state.

Once you feel relaxed, think about the three rays of Awen. See them in your mind's eye. What do the three rays mean to you? What inspiration do they bring into your life? Think not only of their abstract meaning, but also of the three rays as the source of inspiration in your life. Let your mind dwell on this.

Next, think of their literal representation—the sun on the solstices and equinoxes of the year and the turning of the seasons. Think of how this affects your life. Do you follow the wheel of the year in your practices, or do you observe different celebrations? Are you in tune with the natural world, or do you feel separate? Are the solstices and equinoxes important in your life? Think of all these things. Come to know how Awen affects your life.

Once you have learned what you can from this meditation, let your consciousness return to the here and now. Feel relaxed and refreshed as you become aware of your surroundings.

David P. Smith

Chapter 3: Awen and the Natural World

"Nature is my manifestation of God. I go to nature every day for inspiration in the day's work. I follow in building the principles which nature has used in its domain."
(Frank Lloyd Wright)

One of the greatest sources of inspiration, to be found by far, is the natural world. From the songs of birds and the sounds of the wind whispering in the trees to the wonderful beauty of the flora and fauna around us, nature holds nearly limitless inspiration. It has inspired medical, scientific, artistic, and spiritual developments throughout the millennia.

While walking through the forests, over the fields, by the seashore, and many other places, one can find Awen in abundance. One of the best ways to increase the flow of Awen in your life is not only to engage with but also to tune into the natural world. One thing Awen represents is the sun at the equinoxes and solstices, which marks the turning of the wheel of the year and the natural cycles. The ebb and flow of nature around you can become an invaluable source of inspiration within you.

You can grow closer to the natural cycles in many ways: from taking nature walks and caring for a garden to gazing out your window. It is important that you feel the connection; it is not particularly important how you do it. Each of us connects to nature in different ways, and when we make these connections, the power of Awen begins to flow through us and inspire us. If we choose to let it flow, it can help us find a deeper connection within ourselves and with the natural world around us.

Familiarity with nature helps us feel closer to Awen. The reverse is also true: by being close to Awen, we feel closer to nature. Nature and Awen can never be fully separated; they are interconnected within us and throughout the world. Natural beauty will always fill us with awe; likewise, connection to the grand inspiring force that is Awen will also fill us with awe.

As the manifestation of the sun at its solstices and equinoxes, the Awen represents the spinning of the wheel of the year. If your spiritual path follows the wheel of the year and the seasons, you will feel closer to Awen. It is important to remember that Awen is everywhere in nature—it is all around us—and it brings us strength and inspiration. Awen is truly a magical force that helps us not only to learn from nature but also to listen to our own inner guides and voices.

While on our spiritual paths, we are truly on the path of Awen; by following it, we can find wonderful glimpses of truth and wisdom around us. The wisdom of the ages truly exists within us all. We are connected to it—all we need to do is find a way to tap into it. Awen is one way we can do this. We can learn to hear the song of Awen, the song of nature, when we can quiet ourselves long enough to listen to its constant melody.

In my opinion, there are none closer to the Awen naturally than children. They are willing to go outside into nature and let their natural curiosity, imaginations, and creative selves just interact with what is around them. This is something we all should strive to recapture—by letting our creative selves and imaginations interact with nature and Awen—in order to find truth and wisdom in this world and perhaps the next.

Many of us have difficulty connecting to Awen; we not only have separated ourselves from nature but have allowed ourselves to be distracted by the artificially created worlds around us. We sit behind our computers or in front of our televisions—safe little boxes we have created to shelter us from the world outside. We go about our daily routines from house to car, to work, and so on, and we get set in our routines. We often forget—with our busy and distracting lives—to take time to go outside, breathe in the fresh air, and take a little time to connect to the outside world around us.

We often forget, also, that inspiration and joy can be found by communing with others of like minds. When you experience nature with your friends and family, you connect with each other and the world around you. You can see this connection easiest if there are children in your group; watch their wonder at the natural world, and reignite that wonder in yourself. That wonder existed in you until you allowed material things from this world—work, television, and the Internet, to name a few—to distract you from your natural balance and true self.

It is extremely important to take some time to allow the distractions to wane, and let the natural world become a part of your world again. The natural world can be frightening to commune with—due to our own separation from it. As we get closer to it, however, the fear or unsettling feelings will diminish, and we can restore our links to the natural world and our fellow human beings. We will find our full potential as we commune with—and end our distractions and alienation from—nature and each other.

When we close the gaps between ourselves and the natural world, we not only come closer to our natural state, which is how we started eons ago, but also learn how to walk more softly on our planet. This will help to undo any damage we have wrought by being separate. We need to realize that we exist in nature as part of nature. We are not above, below, or separate from nature—we are part of it and the web of life it sustains. Through observing nature and interacting with it, we can learn so much: not only about our world around us but also about ourselves.

Exercise 3: Awen and Nature

Take a nature walk. Be mindful of where you are going and what you are seeing. Look at the trees, flowers, grass, plants, and animals you come across. Do you see anything that inspires you? Why does it inspire you? What does it inspire you to do? Carry a camera with you and take pictures of anything that you find particularly inspiring; these pictures might help inspire you when you cannot actually be outdoors. You may also wish to take a recorder with you and record some of your local nature sounds, which can help remind and inspire you in the future.

Nature Meditation

This meditation is best done out in nature. If you will not be able to meditate outside, try to do this near an open window, or with some nature sounds playing in the background, to help with the visualizations.

Close your eyes. Now become aware of your breathing: in and out, in and out. Become aware of your body; start with your feet and work your way up to your head. As you become aware of each muscle and muscle group, feel them loosen and become completely relaxed. Pause for a moment, and feel your body in its fully relaxed state.

Now visualize yourself in nature. (This is easy if you are already in nature.) Feel the sun on your skin and the wind on your cheek; smell the scents around you and hear all the lovely sounds around you. Let yourself become one with the natural world around you, and let your senses not only be free but also part of that world.

Commune with nature for as long as you wish. Let nature inspire and refresh you. Let your energy mingle with that of the world around you, and the energy of the world mingle with yours. Do not expect anything; just let it flow.

Once you feel that you learned what you can from this meditation, let your consciousness come back to the here and now. Open your eyes. You may find this meditation quite refreshing. Write down your experiences so that you can come back to them at a later time.

David P. Smith

Part 2: Awen and Spirituality

And thus Spoke the Universe...

David P. Smith

Chapter 4: The Light of Your Spirit

"Come forth into the light of things, Let Nature be your teacher."
(William Wordsworth)

When you follow the path of Awen, you are truly following a path of spirit. It guides and directs us as we journey along our spiritual paths. Awen is the divine inspiration that we all seek; it helps us develop our spirituality and improve ourselves as beings.

As we observe nature, take time to meditate, interact with one another, and follow a spiritual path of our choice, we find that we can connect with this divine inspiration. What we do with this connection is wholly up to us as individuals; we can encourage it, ignore it, follow it, or run from it. When we connect with Awen, and choose to follow it, we deepen our spiritual connections and learn much from it. What exactly is learned is often—if not always—individual; it is not something easily shared with another—unless they happen to experience it in the same way.

As human beings, our spirits seem to cry out for meaning; they drive us to find explanations for all the wonderful things around us. We all find this in different ways: through different spiritualities and religions—or through science and rational thought. Some of us find it through a complex interweaving of all three. To truly find what we seek, though, we must look within. When we do this, we find the light that dwells within us all.

We are more than our bodies—we are more than the mere skin that surrounds us—we are spiritual beings. Although we are tethered to this world of form by the bodies in which we currently reside, we go far beyond this. We are beings of radiant light—spiritual and eternal beings. We seek to commune with the world around us on a deeper level and understand why we are here. Many things help us along this path: quieting ourselves, listening to our inner guides and teachers, taking the time to study subjects that appeal to our spirits, and following the divine inspiration that Awen brings to us. We all feel this inspiration; it drives us and helps us to find what we seek—in the ways which will be most meaningful to us. It is truly as individual as our very souls.

Each one of us needs to let our inner light shine out into this world and illuminate everything around us. In all honesty, before we can truly seek the spiritual truths, we must be comfortable in our own skin—and let our inner light shine like a beacon.

We must allow the divine inspiration to find us and guide us to what we seek.

Many of the modern druid groups intone, or chant, the word Awen in their ritual and meditative work. This calls the flowing spirit—the divine inspiration that exists around us—and helps it to join its light to our own. It is intoned normally in three syllables—Ahhh-Oooh-Ennnn—which can also be intoned or repeated as a mantra or meditative tool. It is very similar to the Eastern OM; I have found that Awen and OM can easily be combined and used in meditation.

Invite the light of the Awen in and join it with your light through intonation or chant.This can be an interesting, moving, and guiding experience. When you do this, it can help you connect on a deeper level with the spirit of the Awen and its particular energies and powers. This can be done no matter what religious or spiritual background you follow; it will still be a meaningful and connecting force.

Whether or not you follow this path with a group of like-minded friends, it will always be an individual and interesting path to follow.When we let our inner light shine in groups, then our light can join with the light of those around us; it will shine even brighter than before. So, whether you plan to follow this path alone or with others, know that as individual as this path is, it is also possible to share it with others.

Exercise 4: Working with the Awen Mantra

My work with Awen has led me to try out a mantra during meditation. It has worked well for me; it may work for you as well. In this mantra I intone or sing the eastern OM with the Awen: OM Awen OM, which is intoned as Ommm Aaaaahhhh-Oooooh-Ennnnnn Ommm. When sung, it most often sounds like OM Ahh-ooh-Enn OM; I make sure to sound out all of the syllables. Try using this combination as a meditative tool for a while, and see what it does for you. Start your meditation without focusing on any thoughts—similar to a empty-mind style of meditation. It is okay if thoughts arise, but do not dwell on them; leave them until later. While you are in this state, start intoning or singing the mantra.

Meditation 4: Radiating Your Inner Light

Close your eyes. Now become aware of your breathing: in and out, in and out. Become aware of your body; start with your feet and work your way up to your head. As you become aware of each muscle and muscle group, feel them loosen and become completely relaxed. Pause for a moment, and feel your body in its fully relaxed state.

Now envision a light shining from the center of your being. It starts at your center and begins radiating outward, slowly, until it covers your whole body—inside and out. Now imagine the light growing brighter and brighter. It fills you with light and starts to glow in the environment beyond you; then, it joins with the light in the room and shines out like a beacon. Let your light shine out into the universe, and the light of the universe shine back into you. Feel the light joining with all other light, and you are at its center.

Take some time to feel the light shining out from you and in to you. How does it make you feel? How does it feel to radiate the light within you out to the world? Contemplate the light. How can it bring you the inspiration that you seek?

Once you have learned what you can from this meditation, become aware, once again, of the here and now. Record your experiences in your journal to look at later.

David P. Smith

Chapter 5: The Solar Spirit

"Three things cannot be long hidden: the sun, the moon, and the truth."
(Buddha)

The Awen symbol is also the representation of the sun on the solstices and equinoxes. It is an embodiment of the spirit and energy of the sun that shines down upon us. The sun brings us illumination, energy, the cycles of growth, and warmth. It is an extremely important part of all of our lives; no life, as we know it, would be here without its light and warmth. The ancients saw this as a fact—just as we do today—and they used these specific points to mark the turning of the wheel of the year. It was something they could observe, and by worshipping on these days, they could become connected to the cycles of the seasons.

This reverence for the sun is shown not only by the importance given to the solstices and equinoxes in the ancient calendar but also from Awen's representation of the rays of the sun on the solstices and equinoxes. Modern pagans, especially most modern druid groups, see these as important spiritual days. The sun's strength is ebbing and flowing, and this signifies the changes to come. On the solstices, the sun is at its strongest and weakest points, which mark the longest and shortest days of the year. On the equinoxes, everything is in balance. The solstices and equinoxes generally mark the quarter days—the four main astronomically observable festivals—in the modern pagan Wheel of the Year.

There are also the cross-quarter days, which are based on old Celtic fire festivals: Imbolc, Beltaine, Lughnasadh, and Samhuinn. These festivals all happen at times of the year that mark the changing of the seasons, and they all seem to hinge on the solstices and equinoxes. The wheel turns both in the Northern and Southern Hemispheres, but each festival is opposite to the other, depending on the location.

Northern Hemisphere

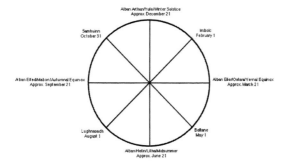

Awen flows down from not only the sun but also the whole of the universe, which brings its divine inspiration and flow into our lives. Through this solar spirit, we are helped to discover our own inner light and inner spirit. By following the ebb and flow of the sun's energies in the solstices and equinoxes, we become more attuned to the natural world around us and strengthen our bond with the Earth, our mother. This in turn leads us to the inspiration and deeper understanding we seek as spiritual beings.

We all must do the work ourselves to grow as spiritual beings. This work cannot be done for us. We can receive help to start our journeys, but no one else can bring us to the end—to the answers we seek. Awen is there to help us and to inspire us along our paths, if we allow it to, and if we truly seek it. It comes and goes as it pleases; sometimes it is strong like the sun on the longest day, and sometimes it is weak like the sun on the shortest day. It is in balance, at other times, as the sun is on the equinoxes.

Exercise 5: Working with the Sun

For this exercise you will need to spend some time out in the sun, so you can feel its energy radiating down. Depending on the time of year, the sun's strength will be different as well as the temperature; there are different lessons to be learned when this exercise is done in different seasons. First, you want to feel the sun as it hits you. How does it feel? Second, you will want to look around and observe how it affects the plants and animals around you. What season is it? Are there flowers in bloom that are turning their faces to the sun? Is it cold? Is the sun barely illuminating a stark winter day? Where do you live, and how does the sun work its magic in your part of the world? Ponder the sun and how it affects you and your personal environment.

Guided Meditation 5: Commune with the Solar Spirit

Close your eyes. Now become aware of your breathing: in and out, in and out. Become aware of your body; start with your feet and work your way up to your head. As you become aware of each muscle and muscle group, feel them loosen and become completely relaxed. Pause for a moment, and feel your body in its fully relaxed state.

Now envision yourself sitting under the sun on a warm spring day. The sun is shining down on you—cleansing and energizing you. Let its energy flow through you: from the crown of your head, through your whole body, and down into the ground below you. Feel this energy; feel yourself become one with this energy. How does it feel? What messages does it carry?

Be open to any images or thoughts that might come to you. Let them flow over you like sunlight and fill you. Once you have learned what you can from this meditation, become aware of your surroundings—of the here and now. Record what you have learned in your journal to look at later.

David P. Smith

Chapter 6: The Universal Spirit

"The cosmos is also within us. We're made of star stuff. We are a way for the cosmos to know itself." (Carl Sagan from Cosmos)

Awen is a great force that exists in this universe—it exists in everything. It is waiting to be found. Every flower, every star, every cloud, every other human being—truly everything—can be a source of this inspiration and is tied to it. By working with Awen and listening to our inner guides, we can come closer to the universal consciousness, the consciousness of divinity.

This universal spirit of Awen manifests in many ways in our lives—through things that seem random, but often are not random at all. These synchronistic moments come into our lives and help us along our paths. These moments can range in quality from meeting a new friend to being awestruck by the beauty around you while on vacation—and much, much more.

The path of Awen is, in an inner sense, a personal journey of self and one's own spirit; however, the universal spirit comes to help us on the way. Sometimes this help can seem like a hindrance, but when followed through to its natural end, it can become the source of some of our greatest inspirations.

The people who come into our lives often teach us

things, even if we never viewed them as teachers. A wonderful example of this is the influence of children. When children are in your life, be they your own children, your nieces and nephews, or even your friend's children, you can learn many things from them. They teach us not only patience but also the importance of play—we should not be so serious all the time. We, as adults, often lose sight of the power of play and of the inner child that exists within us all.

Children see everything in wonder; everything is new and magical to them. Over time this way of looking at the world is lost. This is due—in part—to a variety of influences in our lives. As these influences form us into "responsible" adults, we lose ourselves. We become drones to our everyday work and responsibilities, and too often, we forget that we need to play. We need to keep our sense of wonder and awe of nature so we can see the magic that exists all around us.

When we first enter this world and everything is new, we see the wonder and glory that exists around us in the universe. It sparks our imaginations and fills us with great inspiration and wonder. As children we seem to be closer to the Awen that exists, to the true essence of the universe, and we grow from that in different ways. By learning to reconnect with that, we can truly start to work with Awen; when we do, we will find the inspiration and guidance to grow as spiritual beings.

We often, as adults, lose our sense of imaginative play and even our sense of humor. We let our responsibilities and worries fill our lives and just forget to take time to release, relax, and play. Our spirits need to soar; they need to play and be connected with the world around them. By alienating ourselves from nature and letting ourselves become overly consumed with our worries and responsibilities, we put up a road block between ourselves and the Awen that flows all around us.

This is not to say that we should chuck it all

and forget our responsibilities, but that we need to follow our inner child a bit more—we must take time to play and relax. It is not easy to play and relax in this world—at least not fully—when we face our worries, and especially when we pick up the newspaper or watch the evening news. We must learn to be more comfortable in our own skin and accepting of the other people around us. They, like us, are more than just their skin; they are spiritual beings following wherever their personal paths lead them.

When you connect to the Awen, to this universal spirit, you truly connect to the natural world. This connection also allows you to accept yourself and your fellow human beings. You do not need to see eye-to-eye with everyone; in fact, other people will challenge your own beliefs and sense of self. These challenges can be important to your development, which reinforce your own sense of self. What we need to do is accept that we exist in a wonderful, natural world—a world of which we are a part. We are all made of the same stuff as the rest of the universe. We truly are all connected—on a myriad of levels—and the bond and connection is Awen, which flows within and around us.

Exercise 6: Play

For this exercise, take some time to play—especially with children who might be part of your life in some way. However, if there are no children in your life, learn to play in some other way: from playing in the sand and mud to playing a game of cards. Take time to just slow down, enjoy yourself, and relax. Try to make this a daily, or at least weekly, habit to help you reconnect with that inner child that still exists at your core. This can be extremely helpful on your path to awakening as a spiritual being—and in connecting to the Awen around us. Remember: never take yourself too seriously, have a sense of humor, let yourself laugh at yourself, and have fun.

Guided Meditation 6: Touching the Universal Spirit

Close your eyes. Now become aware of your breathing: in and out, in and out. Become aware of your body; start with your feet and work your way up to your head. As you become aware of each muscle and muscle group, feel them loosen and become completely relaxed. Pause for a moment, and feel your body in its fully relaxed state.

Now take some time and let your mind just wander wherever it wants. Be open to all of the thoughts and images that might flow in. Let the Universal Spirit, and your personal connection to Awen, lead you through it. Take all the time you need, and find all you seek.

Once you have learned what you can from this meditation, let yourself become aware of the here and now. Record your experiences in your journal to look at later. Feel free to repeat this exercise as often as you like; you will notice how things differ from time to time.

Part 3: Awen's Path

David P. Smith

Chapter 7: Starting on the Path

"Do not go where the path may lead, go instead where there is no path and leave a trail."
(Ralph Waldo Emerson)

When you choose to walk down the path of Awen, you choose to be open to the inspiration that flows into your life on a daily basis. Seek out inspiration where it can be found. Allow yourself to go out into nature, play, and get dirty. To walk down the path of Awen means quite a bit, but it truly is your path, and there is no wrong way to approach it. Once you have decided to walk down the path of Awen, you have begun.

Some people find Awen through nature alone, some find it through working with ritual, and still others find it through meditation. It is available to us on many levels and avenues, and in many cases, it comes in all of these modalities and more. Many things will change as you walk this path; you will find out much about yourself and the world around you.

To follow the way of Awen is to follow the song of your soul as it joins in the symphony of life. Each of us sounds our notes and choruses in this great symphony of life that plays continuously. The real secret here is twofold: it is not only finding our inspiration but also our way to hear this song that exists around us. Again, this can be done in many ways; I found the best way is to find time to quiet yourself, and just listen.

We live in a world of noise and distractions. Many of us tend to talk more than we listen. Sometimes, if we take the time to listen to each other, and the world around us, we can learn quite a bit about what is going on around us—and in the minds of our fellow human beings. We all need not only to be heard, but also to share what we feel with others. Sometimes, though, we need to listen so that others can get that release as well.

There are no gurus on this path. There are occasional guides, and our own inner guides, who will be there to help us along our way. We truly must blaze our own paths to find what Awen means to us and what we need to do to access it in our own lives. By making it part of our lives, we are inviting inspiration to all levels of our lives.

Awen affects our lives in so many ways: spiritually, emotionally, physically, psychologically, and energetically. To walk down the path of Awen is a true voyage of discovery—of self and the world around us. I hope that you find working with Awen as rewarding and fulfilling as I have.

Exercise 7: Where Does Your Path Start?

For this exercise, it is important to look at yourself. Looking within is one way each one of us can find inspiration and calm. Find a special or inspiring place—perhaps near the ocean or in a local park—to sit quietly for a while. Just take some time to think about what inspires you: what inside you calls out for this inspiration? It may take several attempts, but when you find this inner drive, you will know that you have truly started on the path.

Guided Meditation 7: A Path Ever Winding

Close your eyes. Now become aware of your breathing: in and out, in and out. Become aware of your body; start with your feet and work your way up to your head. As you become aware of each muscle and muscle group, feel them loosen and become completely relaxed. Pause for a moment and feel your body in its fully relaxed state.

Now envision yourself at the start of a pathway. It may wind through a wood, run along a cliff face, lead onward towards a beach, or be a simple path of paving stones—whatever you wish it to be and whatever holds the most power for you. See this path as a new direction in your life, and feel the call of inspiration coming from it. This is truly your own path to follow, and along it, you will find things that inspire and strike you with awe. The further down the path you go, the longer it seems to stretch in front of you. This path will take a lifetime to find the end of.

If it feels right, take the first steps on the path. Note what you see, what surrounds you, and how it makes you feel. There is no right or wrong way to do this; do it in a way that you feel comfortable with, and be sure to make it your own. Let this be as personal to you as anything can be.

Here is a place you can retreat and find the inspiration that calls to your very soul. You can also come here to review where you have tread on this path before, and rest as you prepare to make your way further down the path.

Once you have learned what you can from this meditation, and you have truly made it your own, return to the here and now. Record how this makes you feel and what you saw in your journal for later contemplation.

Chapter 8: Further along the Path

"As a single footstep will not make a path on the earth, so a single thought will not make a pathway in the mind. To make a deep physical path, we walk again and again. To make a deep mental path, we must think over and over the kind of thoughts we wish to dominate our lives."

(Henry David Thoreau)

The further you travel down this path, the longer the path becomes, stretching ever onwards. The path of Awen is a lifelong journey. Once you have found your inner Awen and started following its path, it will wind onward and onward until the end of your journey—and perhaps beyond. In following this path, you are striving to connect yourself to nature and the divine essence that exists within and around us. This inspiration can move us to do wonderful things; it can help us along the various paths we all walk throughout this lifetime.

There are many gifts Awen inspires—artistic, intellectual, or otherwise. Awen truly is a place of birth and rebirth. Through Awen, and our own conscious efforts, we can bring many things into creation—from wondrous music and works of art to inspired works of nonfiction such as this book. To be open enough to let the Awen work through you spontaneously—that is an amazing feeling.

Rituals, books, paintings, songs, poems, gardens, prayers, dances, and perhaps even our children are all the creations of Awen; all can inspire its flow. It flows around us like the waves of the sea. It brings us the floods of realization and inspiration we need at the times we need them—though not always when we want them. All we can do is be open to these times when the Awen shines down upon us, filling our spirits with the inspiration that brings forth the creation of so many things. We all have our ways of experiencing this—and our own ways of expressing it. On this path, you will find your own experience and expression of this wonderful inspiration—brought forth from the divine around and within us.

As I have stated before, there are many ways to connect with Awen—from listening to music and looking at works of art to connecting with the natural world around us. Some ways work better for certain people than others; for me, it is a blend of many of them. I draw great inspiration not only from others' works, but also from sunshine and druidic ritual to mark the seasons.

The further down this path you decide to tread, the more things you may find inspiration in—as long as you are open to this inspiration. The methods and exercises that are within the pages of this book are just little things that can help along the way—and all of them can be adapted so that they fit best to you and your own path. This is a voyage of discovery over the seas of inspiration, and if you have chosen to walk this path, you will find many rewards—and perhaps even some pitfalls.

It is easy to become distracted along this path, easy to lose focus. There are many things that are breathtakingly inspirational, but as we begin to see, some can even skew our view of the real world around us. As "The Cauldron Born," a song by Damh the Bard says: "Through the illusion and into the dream!" We must strive to keep our feet planted firmly on the ground, while allowing our heads to float free in the clouds. This is a pitfall of many spiritual paths—letting yourself become more engrossed in the next world, or other worlds, and not allowing yourself to live here, in the now. Use your normal routines and necessities to temper all the work you do with inspiration.

The rewards you find will surely bring joy into your life. When you incorporate the lessons that the inspiration provides for you into your being—in the here and now—it is truly a marvelous thing. You may even be moved to share your works of inspiration with your friends, family, or the world at large; in fact, I encourage you to do this. Inspiration brings forth more inspiration. What you have created from your inspiration might just inspire others and help them along their paths.

Although the path of Awen is truly an individual path, the interactions you have with others can influence both your own path and theirs. Share your joy, your love, and your passion as much as you wish to. When you share forth positivity, you will reap it back one hundred fold, if not more. Once the light of Awen shines down on your path and you start seeing the inspiration all around you, you will perceive even the most common things in a different light.

Exercise 8: Create

The title of this exercise essentially states the whole purpose of this exercise. For this you need to create something. Use whatever you like, and create whatever you like. Find something that inspires you; when you do, create a drawing or a poem about it, or take an artistic picture of it, or make up a song or dance about it. Do whatever you personally feel comfortable with. Let the inspiration flow through you and take note of exactly how it makes you feel during the act of creation. We all have our own talents—use your own talents or explore something new while doing this. Most of all: enjoy and have fun.

Guided Meditation 8: Where Does Your Path Lead?

This particular meditation may work best if repeated over time; its repetition may bring forth new ideas and revelations to you.

Close your eyes. Now become aware of your breathing: in and out, in and out. Become aware of your body; start with your feet and work your way up to your head. As you become aware of each muscle and muscle group, feel them loosen and become completely relaxed. Pause for a moment and feel your body in its fully relaxed state.

Now take some time to look back at the path your life has taken thus far. You can start from last week, or all the way back to birth. Take as long as you need and look back at whatever you wish. If something in the past inspired you, you may wish to take a moment to focus on that, but then return to reviewing your path.

Once you feel you have reviewed enough of your path, or your review has returned to the present, take the time to look toward the future. Where would you like your path to lead you in the future? What would you like to see brought to creation in your life? How can Awen's inspiration and your perspiration work together to make this a reality? You can meditate on this as lightly or as deeply as you like.

Once you have a good image of where you would like your path to lead, let your consciousness flow back to the here and now. Record in your journal about your experiences and review them—especially if you repeat this exercise.

Chapter 9: Claiming Your Path

"Impart as much as you can of your spiritual being to those who are on the road with you, and accept as something precious what comes back to you from them."
(Albert Schweitzer)

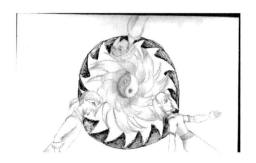

The path of Awen truly influences us on all levels, once we choose to walk it. What you have read within the pages of this book is here to give you a taste of what walking this path can be like.

If you wish to claim this path, you need to make it totally yours. Though you will come to accept some influences to it, such as this book, it is yours and yours alone. Only you can claim this path; Awen can guide you, as can others, but the true path lies within. Though the path of Awen has been walked by many throughout the ages, under one name or another, each individual's path is slightly different.

Go, with your inner guides, into the wild places where Awen lives and blaze your own trail down the path. When you walk onward and create the trail as you go, you make it your own. My experiences are not your experiences—I can explain how Awen affects me, but it is not the same as living the experience yourself. You must truly let your own inner Awen flow—if you believe this path is right for you.

I have thoroughly enjoyed writing these pages and sharing my own views on Awen with you. Take from it what you will, and go make your own way down the path—if that is what you wish to do. May the Awen flow to and through you, and may you find the inspiration you seek along your path.

Exercise 9: Make It Your Own

For this exercise, if you wish to follow it, create your own exercise. Draw from anything you have done thus far, or completely make it up yourself. It is your path. Now lead yourself on it.

Guided Meditation 9: Your Own

Just as you created your own exercise for this chapter, this is your opportunity to create your own guided meditation. You can use the format I have used, or some other format you have learned in your seeking. All that is required is that you make it yourself. It is time to be your own guide on the path. Enjoy!

If you have questions, or want to share your experiences or thoughts, you can e-mail the author at awenspath@@cox.net

About the Author

Rev. David P. Smith was born on November 3, 1977. In 1999, he received his bachelor of arts degree in Psychology and Religious Studies from Salve Regina University. David is a practicing Druid Priest and member of many druidic organizations: the Order of

Bards, Ovates, and Druids; the Ancient Order of Druids in America; the Reformed Druids of Gaia; the British Druid Order; and the Henge of Keltria. He spends most of his life as a seeker, to try to find himself and enhance his spiritual development. He is very interested in all forms of religion and spirituality. When not working and studying, David likes to travel to sacred places around the Earth and spend time with his loving wife and son. He currently resides in Rhode Island.

Druidic Orders

Ancient Order of Druids in America
P.O. Box 996,
Cumberland, MD 21501
http://www.aoda.org

Ár nDraíocht Féin: A Druid Fellowship
P.O. Box 17874
Tuscon, AZ 85731-7874
http://www.adf.org

The British Druid Order
BDO Midlands
PO Box 6733
Bridgnorth WV16 9BW
Shropshire, UK
http://www.druidry.co.uk

The Henge of Keltria
2350 Spring Road, PMB-140
Smyrna, GA 30080-2630
http://www.keltria.org

The Order of Bards, Ovates, and Druids
PO Box 1333
Lewes, East Sussex BN7 1DX, UK
http://www.druidry.org

The Order of the Mithril Star
P.O. Box 6753
Eureka, CA 95502-6753
http://www.mithrilstar.org

Reformed Druids of Gaia (RDG)
http://www.reformed-druids.org

Reformed Druids of North America (RDNA)
http://www.rdna.info

Recommended Reading on Druidry and Related Studies

the Bard, Hugin. *A Bard's Book of Pagan Songs: Stories and Music from the Celtic World*. St. Paul, MN: Llewellyn Publications, 2002.

Baxter, Nicola. *Celtic Tales and Legends: Ten Mystical Stories Retold for Children*. Leicester: Armadillo, 2012.

Blamires, Steve. *Celtic Tree Mysteries: Practical Druid Magic and Divination*. St. Paul, MN: Llewellyn Publications, 2003.

———. *Glamoury: Magic of the Celtic Green World*. St.Paul, MN: Llewellyn Publications, 1995.

Caesar, Julius. *Caesar: The Gallic War*. Loeb Classical Library. Translated by H.J. Edwards. Cambridge, MA: Harvard University Press, 1917.

Caldecott, Moyra. *Women in Celtic Myth: Tales of Extraordinary Women from Ancient Celtic Tradition*. Rochester, VT: Inner Traditions, 1992.

Carr-Gomm, Philip. *Druidcraft: The Magic of Wicca*

and Druidry. HaperCollins Canada, 2002.

———. *The Druid Renaissance: The Voice of Druidry Today*. London: Thorsons, 1996.

———. *The Druid Way: A Journey through an Ancient Landscape*. Rockport, ME: Element Books, 1993.

———. *Elements of the Druid Tradition*. Rockport, ME: Element Books, 1991.

———. *In The Grove of the Druids: The Druid Teachings of Ross Nichols*. London: Watkins Publishing, 2002.

Carr-Gomm, Philip and Stephanie Carr-Gomm, *The Druid Animal Oracle: Working with the Sacred Animals of the Druid Tradition*. New York: Simon & Schuster, 1994.

———. *The Druid Plant Oracle: Working with the Magical Flora of the Druid Tradition*. New York: St. Martin's Press, 2008.

Conway, D.J. *By Oak, Ash, and Thorn: Modern Celtic Shamanism*. St. Paul, MN: Llewellyn Publications, 1995.

———. *Celtic Magic*. St. Paul, MN: Llewellyn

Publications, 1990.

Cowan, Tom Dale. *Fire in the Head: Shamanism and the Celtic Spirit*. New York: HarperCollins, 1993.

Cunliffe, Barry. *The Ancient Celts*. London: Penguin Books, 1999.

Ellison, Robert Lee. *Ogham: The Secret Language of the Druids*. Tucson, AZ: ADF Publishing, 2007.

———. *The Solitary Druid: Walking the Path of Wisdom and Spirit*. New York: Citadel Press, 2005.

Garner, Alan. *The Owl Service*. London: Lions, 1973.

Green, Miranda Jane. *Celtic Myths*. Austin, TX: University of Texas Press, 1993.Teach Yourself Celtic Myths by Steve Eddy and Claire Hamilton

Greer, John Michael. *The Druidry Handbook: Spiritual Practice Rooted in the Living Earth*. York Beach, ME: Red Wheel/Weiser, 2006.

Guest, Charlotte E., trans. *The Mabinogion*. Mineloa, NY: Dover Publications, 1997.

Guyonvarc'h, Christian J. *The Making of a Druid:*

Hidden Teachings from the Colloquy of Two Sages. Translated by Clare Marie Frock. Rochester, VT: Inner Traditions, 2002.

Heinlein, Robert A. *Stranger in a Strange Land*. New York: Ace Books, 1991.

Herm, Gerhard. *The Celts*. New York: St. Martin's Press, 2002.

Hesse, Hermann. *Siddhartha*. Translated by Hilda Rosner. New York: Bantam Books, 1971.

Hopman, Ellen Evert. *A Druid's Herbal for the Sacred Earth Year*. Rochester, VT: Destiny Books, 1995.

Howe, E. Graham. *The Mind of a Druid*. London: Skoob, 1989.

Jones, Leslie Ellen. *Druid, Shaman, Priest: Metaphors of Celtic Paganism*. Enfield Lock, Middlesex, UK: Hisarlik Press, 1998.

Knight, Sirona. *Celtic Traditions: Druids, Faeries, and Wiccan Rituals*. New York: Citadel Press, 2000.

Kondratiev, Alexei. *The Apple Branch: A path to Celtic Ritual*. Cork [Ireland]: Collins Press, 1998.

Le Braz, Anatole. *Celtic Legends of the Beyond: A Celtic Book of the Dead*. Translated by Derek Bryce. York Beach, ME: Samuel Weiser, 1999.

Malory, Thomas. *Le Morte D'Arthur: Complete, Unabridged, Illustrated Edition*. Edited by John Matthews. London: Cassell Illustrated, 2003.

Markale, Jean. *The Druids: Celtic Priests of Nature*. Translated by Jon Graham. Rochester, VT: Inner Traditions, 1999.

Matthews, Caitlin. *The Celtic Book of the Dead: A Guide for Your Voyage to the Celtic Otherworld*. New York: St. Martin's Press, 1992.

Matthews, Caitlin and John Matthews. *Walkers between the Worlds: the Western Mysteries from Shaman to Magus*. Rochester, VT: Inner Traditions, 2003.

Matthews, John. *The Bardic Source Book: Inspirational Legacy and Teaching of the Ancient Celts*. London: Blandford, 1998.

———, ed., *The Celtic Seers' Source Book: Vision and*

Magic in the Druid

Tradition. London: Cassell Illustrated, 1999.

———, ed., *The Druid Source Book*. New York: Sterling Publishing, 1998.

———. *The Green Man: Spirit of Nature*. Boston, MA: Red Wheel, 2011.

———, ed., *Secrets of the Druids*. NY: Black Dog & Leventhal, 2002.

———. *The Sidhe: Wisdom from the Celtic Otherworld*. Issaquah, WA: Lorian Association, 2004.

McBratney, Sam. *Celtic Myths*. London: Hodder & Stoughton, 2004.

McCoy, Edain. *Celtic Myth and Magic: Harness the Power of the Gods and Goddesses*. St. Paul, MN: Llewellyn Publications, 2002.

Myers, Brendan Cathbad. *The Mysteries of Druidry: Celtic Mysticism, Theory, and Practice*. Franklin Lakes, NJ: New Page Books, 2006.

Nichols, Ross. *The Book of Druidry*. New York: Castle Books, 2009.

Orr, Emma Restall. *Druidry*. London: Thorsons, 2001.

———. *Principles of Druidry: The Only Introduction You'll Ever Need (Thorsons Principles Series)*. London: Thorsons, 1998.

Piggott, Stuart. *The Druids*. New York: Thames & Hudson, 1985.

Shallcross, Philip. *Druidry*. London: Little, Brown Book Group, 2000.

Smith, David P. *Honoring the Sacred Earth: A Path to Spiritual Enlightenment*. Rockville, MD: Dreamz-Work Productions, 2010.

———. *Under An Expanse of Oaks: A Druid's Journey*. Rockville, MD: Dreamz-Work Productions, 2009.

Squire, Charles. *Mythology of Ancient Britain and Ireland*. Whitefish, MT: Kessinger Publishing, 2003.

———. *Celtic Myths and Legends*. New York: Random House Value Publishing, 1997.

Steiner, Rudolf. *The Druids: Esoteric Wisdom of the Ancient Celtic Priests*. Forest Row, East Sussex:

Rudolf Steiner Press, 2002.

Stewart, Mary. *The Merlin Trilogy*. New York: Morrow, 1980.

Stewart, R.J. *Celtic Gods, Celtic Goddesses*. London: Cassell Illustrated, 1992.

Sutton, Maya Magee and Nicholas R. Mann. Druid Magic: The Practice of Celtic Wisdom. St. Paul, MN: Llewellyn Publications, 2008.

White, T.H. *The Once and Future King*. New York: Ace Books, 1987.

Wolfe, Amber. *Druid Power: Celtic Faerie Craft and Elemental Magic*. St. Paul, MN: Llewellyn Publications, 2004.

Yeats, William Butler, ed., *Treasury of Irish Myth, Legend, and Folklore*. New York: Crown Publishers, 1986.

Web Resources

1. "Symbols of Druid Identity," Isaac and Phaedra Bonewits' Neopagan.net, last modified April 20, 2011, http://www.neopagan.net/DruidSymbols. html.

2. "Awen," The Nexus Druids, accessed December 16, 2012, http://www.freewebs.com/nexusdruids/ awen (site is moving to https://sites.google.com/site/nexusdruids/ tomes-of-the-earth/awen).

3. Grant, Angela, "A Short History of the Awen," The Druid Network, accessed December 16, 2012, http://druidnetwork.org/beliefs/articles/ kestrel.

4. The Order of Bards, Ovates, and Druids, last updated December 10, 2012, http://www.duidry.org.

David P. Smith

Bibliography

Ab Ithel, J. Williams, ed., *The Barddas of Iolo Morganwyg Vol. I*. London: D.J. Roderick, 1862.

Billington, Penny. *The Path of Druidry: Walking the Ancient Green Way*. Woodbury, MN: Llewellyn Publications, 2011.

Carr-Gomm, Phillip. *Elements of the Druid Tradition*. Rockport, ME: Element Books, 1991.

Griffith. *The Welsh Question and Druidism*. London: Robert Banks & Son, 1887.

Myers, Brendan Cathbad. *The Mysteries of Druidry: Celtic Mysticism, Theory, and Practice*. Franklin Lakes, NJ: New Page Books, 2006.

Smith, David. *Under An Expanse of Oaks: A Druid's Journey*. Rockville, MD: Dreamz-Work Productions, 2009.

Stewart, R.J. and Williamson, Robin. *Celtic Bards, Celtic Druids*. London: Blandford, 1999.

Talboys, Graeme. *Way of the Druid: Renaissance of a Celtic Religion and Its Relevance*. New York. John Hunt Publishing, 2005.

Image Credits

Cover art by: Lusete

Section art by: Rev. David P. Smith

Chapter beginnings art by: Ivy Basley

Awen on Oak by George Rix

Other Books By the Author

http://oaklightpublishing.com